THE HIDDEN
FEMINISM, WOMEN
IN IRELAND

UNDERCURRENTS Series Editor J.J. Lee

The Hidden Tradition: Feminism, Women and Nationalism in Ireland

CAROL COULTER

CORK UNIVERSITY PRESS

For Betty Hamilton

First published in 1993 by
Cork University Press
University College
Cork

© Carol Coulter 1993
Reprinted in 1994

British Library Cataloguing in Publication Data

A CIP catalogue record for this book is available from the British Library

ISBN 0 902561 72 3

Typeset in Ireland by Seton Music Graphics Ltd, Co. Cork
Printed in Ireland by ColourBooks, Baldoyle, Co. Dublin

CONTENTS

ACKNOWLEDGEMENTS

I would like to thank the following: Nuala O'Faolain for suggesting I write this book; Stasia Crickley, Mary Cullen, Jo Kennedy and Mary Maher for their invaluable information and insights; Karen Carlton and Kathleen Delap for their help with the history of the Irish Countrywomen's Association; Bride Rosney; and, for their helpful comments on the text, Imelda Brophy, Harry Browne, Liz Butler-Cullingford, Sandra Cooke, John Daly, Declan Kiberd, David Lloyd and Harry Vince.

Carol Coulter
October 1993

1. INTRODUCTION

The election of Mary Robinson as President of Ireland in November 1990 was widely welcomed as a triumph for those who supported a modernising, liberal agenda for Ireland, and as a defeat for those associated with nationalism and Catholic traditionalism. The growth in her popularity since her election is seen as further evidence of support for what she is held to represent. This is linked in recent comment with the defeat of the Government's latest Constitutional amendment on abortion, attempting to further restrict access to abortion in the light of a Supreme Court ruling that it could be available when the mother's life was threatened, and the publication of the long-awaited Second Report of the Commission on the Status of Women.

Yet anyone who has seen Robinson among the people of rural Ireland, or in the country's inner city communities, must doubt this simple interpretation of the significance of her election. While no-one can deny her outstanding record as a lawyer and champion of women through the avenue of the courts, or her role in sponsoring liberal legislation on issues like contraception, it is clear that this is not what she means to many of the thousands who work to transform their villages, towns and neighbourhoods in anticipation of her visits, who flock to hear her speak, who seek the sanctification of her presence at cultural and community events. Indeed, so much an icon has she become that it now seems almost blasphemous to utter a word of criticism of her, and her erstwhile opponents have been, without exception, silent. (All this changed with her visit, in June 1993, to West Belfast, when significant sections of the political class criticized her, though not, as far as can be ascertained, the mass of ordinary people. The reasons for this are gone into below.)

This unprecedented popularity of a political figure has much to do with Robinson's personal qualities – her evident honesty and integrity, her intelligence and education which make her a worthy

1

representative abroad – but these alone do not explain it. The fact that she is a woman, and a woman in such a representative role, has not only transformed people's attitude to the presidency, as she set out to do; it has also allowed access, through her, to another kind of politics, marginalised and driven underground by the institutional politics in operation since the foundation of the state, but alive in the recesses of popular memory. This kind of politics – decentralised, communalist, responsive to local demands and needs – has a profound, if not always amicable, relationship with Ireland's nationalist tradition.

It has become commonplace in modern debate in Ireland to suggest that nationalism and feminism are opposites, one a patriarchal ideology rooted in traditional Catholicism, the subordination of women and an idealisation of the past, the other a secular, modern, international outlook which will play an important role in emancipating Ireland from the shackles of its obsessions with the past and allow it to take its place among the nations of the new Europe. The latter view is often accompanied by the assumption that the feminist movement began in Ireland in 1970 with the foundation of the modern Irish women's movement, and that prior to that Irish women lived as the prisoners of tradition, obscurantism, ignorance and servitude to men.

It is true that some feminist scholars challenge that view, and have done important work on the role of women in the nationalist and suffrage movements at the beginning of the century. But even then it is accepted that women not only departed from the political scene with the foundation of the Irish state, but disappeared virtually without trace, so that the movement born in the 1970s sprang into being without any obvious antecedents. (Hilda Tweedy's account of the history of the Irish Housewives' Association is the first major contribution which challenges this.) Further, the emergence of Irish women onto the national political stage at the beginning of the century is seen as coming from nowhere, a feminist flash in the pan which disappeared as soon as the male project of state formation was achieved.

But did those women of the early twentieth century come from nowhere? And did they and their daughters disappear? Or is there a subterranean tradition in this country of women's rebellion and incursion into public life, of which that early movement, and the recent election of Mary Robinson, are but the most visible manifestations?

I would argue the latter, that those politically active women of the early twentieth century came out of a pre-existing tradition of women's involvement in nationalist struggle, that this offered them scope for a wider range of activities in public life than that experienced by their sisters in imperialist countries, and that all this was then closed off to them by the newly-formed patriarchal state, modelled essentially on its colonial predecessor.

Not only in Ireland, but throughout the colonised world, women came onto the public stage in large numbers through the great nationalist movements of the beginning of this century. Their experience of political activity, and its extent, differed from that of women in the imperialist countries because of the space created by the existence of mass nationalist movements, the widespread rejection of existing political institutions and culture, and the different family relationships which existed in colonial countries.

However, their involvement in the revolutionary movements was not matched by their place in the newly-created states. Like the poorer sections of the society, they found themselves excluded from political life in the new state, which usually established its own specific form of patriarchy, combining the institutional patriarchy of the former regime with all the most conservative elements of local religious and cultural traditions.

Women's organisational skills and commitment to their immediate communities did not disappear, however, but found new ways of expressing themselves within the confines of the new regimes. Although often cloaked in tradition, women found ways of fighting their oppression and for the improvement of the lives of their families and communities, using apparently conventional organisations like, in Ireland, the Irish Countrywomen's Association and the Irish Housewives' Association. The space for women's activity in the community was thus extended. Emigration and poverty also impelled women, including unorganised women, to play central roles in their families and communities.

Western feminism has left most women in formerly colonial countries virtually untouched, and indeed is viewed with suspicion in some cultures. However, the reinterpretation of tradition and of women's roles has been used extensively in such countries, notably in Latin America and the Middle East, to extend the space for women's involvement in public life and in efforts to transform their societies, sometimes with dramatic results. The experiences of such women should promote a re-evaluation of the relationship between feminism and nationalism, feminism and tradition and feminism and religion.

Finally, I would argue that the emergence of community-based women's groups in all parts of this country is of the greatest significance to the future of the women's movement – and to the broader political culture – here. It has been to this that Mary Robinson appealed during her campaign, and to which she regularly returns in her trips around the country. It was the work of such groups which prompted her controversial visit to West Belfast, and in her own speeches she has pointed to their global significance.

In the nationalist areas of the North such groups form a network of organisations that offer an implicit alternative to state structures, and as such have a literally subversive content. They have not reached this level in the southern state, mainly because the state is not regarded with the same hostility there, but they contain that potential, especially in areas of great social alienation. The socially radical, decentralising impulse which many of its women activists brought to the early nationalist movement in Ireland may yet come into its own.

2. NATIONALISM, RELIGION AND THE FAMILY

The involvement of women is a common feature of nationalist movements. From India to Egypt to Africa to Ireland, the upsurge of nationalism was accompanied by the emergence of women onto the streets in public protest and into public life as organisers, leaders and shock troops. The fact that these societies were often criticised by the imperialist power as repressive of their women, keeping them in thrall to religious and cultural practices redolent of a benighted past, makes this involvement all the more interesting and significant.

Indeed, women have played a greater role, by and large, in the first part of this century in those countries which have sought to end the domination of a colonial power than they have in many Western European countries. While the suffrage movement was very important in these countries, the number of women actively involved was relatively small. Yet in India, for example, the number of women involved in Gandhi's salt marches ran to millions. Of the 80,000 arrested during these marches, 17,000 were women.[1]

The similarities between the different experiences are striking. While the women participated as women, and often formulated specific demands relating to their special interest in the welfare of their families, they saw themselves as an integral part of the emerging nation, with no aims distinct from those of the emancipation of the people as a whole. Indeed, one of the problems of nationalism is the manner in which all the diverse groups swept up in the emancipatory surge which accompanies a nationalist uprising articulate their often contradictory demands as part of a single movement.

In India, when the male leaders of the civil disobedience campaign in the 1930s were imprisoned, the women took over the running of the campaign, exactly as the Ladies' Committee had taken on some of the work of the jailed Fenian leaders in Ireland in the

1860s, and as the Ladies' Land League took on the role of the Land League 20 years later. Jawaharlal Nehru later related his father's astonishment at his mother's behaviour, because he and his friends had 'in no way encouraged these aggressive activities of women all over the country'.[2]

There were political demonstrations by women in Egypt from the early years of the twentieth century, and women were killed in anti-government demonstrations. Again, they saw themselves as part of a movement led by their menfolk: 'We, the women of Egypt, mothers, sisters and wives of those who have been the victims of British greed and exploitation . . . deplore the brutal, barbarous actions that have fallen upon . . . the Egyptian nation. Egypt has committed no crime except to express her desire for independence', read the petition organised by Huda Sharawi, wife of the founder of Wafd and herself the founder of the Egyptian Feminist Union.[3]

In Algeria women broke with their traditional role in the family to join the *maqui*[4] and participated in the fight for independence throughout black Africa.[5] In all these countries their hopes for equal treatment after independence were dashed as the new state was established, modelled to a greater or lesser extent on that which it had replaced.

It was Nehru who most perceptively saw the dual content of women's involvement in the nationalist movement:

> They were mostly middle class women, accustomed to a sheltered life, and suffering chiefly from the many repressions and customs produced by a society dominated to his own advantage by man. The call of freedom had always a double meaning for them, and the enthusiasm and energy with which they threw themselves into the struggle had no doubt their springs in the vague and hardly conscious, but nevertheless intense, desire to rid themselves of domestic slavery also.[6]

It is my belief that women were able to play such an important role in nationalist movements because of the difference between the experience of the family and religion in colonial countries and that within the colonising countries of Europe.[7]

Religion and resistance

The religious traditions of India, especially Hinduism, were invoked to justify the involvement of women in the movement for independence, although the thrust of the movement was secular. Usually the Western-educated middle class formulated a nationalist, secular ideology modelled on the principles of the European Enlightenment, while the more oppressed layers of peasants, small traders and workers, less assimilated into the culture of the colonial power, found their own forms of revolt, nurtured by indigenous culture and folk tradition. It was this mass base to the resistance that gave it its power.

Religion has a particular potency in countries with a colonial past, where secularism has been an aspect of the ideology of the coloniser rather than an indigenous product. Religion sanctifies the moments of significance in human lives – birth, passage to adulthood, marriage, death. All of these moments are celebrated within the context of the family, marking, as they do, points in its evolution. Religion also provides rituals for the mundane routines of family and community life – the marking of the seasons, the preparation of food. Further, religion serves as a bridge between the family and the broader community, especially when the community is denied expression as a civic entity in an independent nation. And, as blacks in the southern states of the US will remember, it can provide powerful allegories for the experience of suffering and the hope of emancipation when these cannot be expressed in an overtly political form. Therefore in these situations religious convictions and religious imagery often play an important part in resistance movements.

In most countries dominated by colonialism, resistance has been led by a section of the native middle class which acquired the education of the occupier, including its rhetoric of enlightenment and democracy, which was then applied to the situation of their own emerging nations. Modern nationalism is, above all, a European creation, and the dawn of nationalism in Western Europe in the eighteenth century is linked by Benedict Anderson with the dusk of religion.[8]

However, European ideologies always suffer a transformation when they are exported to the colonies. The secular nationalism which first attracted the young intellectuals of the colonies was quickly combined with a rediscovery of and a reassertion of pride in the native culture, which was often homogenised and idealised in the process, its more conservative aspects enhanced. This went with the discovery, both culturally and as a political force, of the peasantry and, sometimes, the urban poor, who were used by the emerging new élite, which then consolidated a new state perpetuating the inequalities of the old.

This demanded the creation of an ideology to justify the new *status quo*. The native culture, inherently uncentralised, further fragmented by years of foreign domination, is given an artificial centralisation and cohesion to serve the conservative needs of the new rulers.[9] The diverse, chaotic and often subversive aspects of the indigenous culture are purged in the name of a new 'national' culture, inculcated by the education system, and combined with a new version of history to justify the new *status quo*. Usually the religion of the mass of the people is pressed into service to assist in this role. This proves a potent instrument for social control, especially the oppression of women.

In India, for example, the model Gandhi proposed for Indian women was Sita, the chaste, self-sacrificing wife of the Hindu god Rama. But there also existed a powerful cult of Draupadi, the strong-willed, passionate, polyandrous wife of the five Pandavas of the Mahabharata. She is the subject of poems by the South Indian

Tamil poet Subraminiya Bharathi, but is not exalted by official ideology.[10] Commentators have pointed out that Gandhi's model of Sita had more to do with Victorian ideals of womanhood than with Hindu tradition.

> While highlighting and legally abolishing the worst excesses . . . emphasising female education and mobilising women for *satyagraha* [peaceful resistance] the movement gave the illusion of change while women were kept within the structural confines of family and society. . . . Women in the nationalist struggle did not use the occasion to raise issues that affected them as women.[11]

Nonetheless, religion remains an important part of national culture, or cultures, when the nation is being formed from diverse elements. It has often been a badge of separateness from the occupier, offering a sense of moral superiority in the midst of social inferiority and transcendental salvation when there was no sign of a temporal one. It is not surprising that in many former colonies women seek to reinterpret, rather than reject, the religion they were brought up with.

The family in colonial society

For women in Western Europe who sought a role in civic life at the end of the eighteenth century the biggest obstacle was society, based on the family, which sanctioned their subordination to men within the family by depriving them of access to education and the means for an independent life.[12] The debate which took place about the role of women concentrated on whether or not they were fit to assume an equal role, or whether they were essentially suited to playing a subordinate role to men within the family, a microcosm of the hierarchical structure on which their society is built. This debate has continued for two hundred years.

However, the experience of women in countries dominated by colonialism was different. Their public and civic life was dominated by an outsider, who forcibly occupied that space. Those excluded from it were excluded by reason of colour, language, religion or other mark of origin and distinctness from the occupier. The exclusion was two-fold: the occupier not only took over the administration (and often ownership) of the colony; he allowed the native access to it only to the extent to which he (and only *he*) was prepared to adopt the language and ways of the occupier.

So public space became alien for all the native inhabitants. It was a space where they had to proclaim their own culture and language inferior. To take a place in it they had to betray themselves in some essential way. Yet doing so was, for some, necessary for survival.

The family, however, was different. In the family one could speak one's own language, practise one's own customs, express one's own opinions, be oneself. It was an inviolate space, the one place where the occupier could not enter – at least, not without doing violence to his own rhetoric on the sanctity of the family. Small wonder, therefore, that the family sometimes became the locus of resistance to the occupier.

Thus the family could become the crucible of rebellion, the training ground for a generation of revolutionaries, as the history of Irish nationalism attests. A perennial feature of contemporary Irish politics is the role played by 'political families', where one generation succeeds another in party and public life. This has far less to do with nepotism than it does with the tradition of nationalist politics, which goes back to the eighteenth century and the United Irishmen, where children were reared within an ideology of political rebellion, where the family was organised around the need for solidarity with those victimised because of it, and where political agreement was more a prerequisite for marriage than the more conventional requirements of property and position. (The negative side of this, of course, is the dynastic element in the politics of countries with a colonial history, of which Ireland and India provide just two examples.)

Given the necessity for internal solidarity within families with a tradition of rebellion, the distinction between male and female roles could become blurred. At any time the women, as much as the men, could be required to suffer privation, to withstand interrogation, to sustain the family alone. This inevitably affected the attitudes towards gender roles of both women and men. Therefore in the writings of women involved in the nationalist movement we find an assumption of equality with men, even if, by the beginning of the twentieth century, this was combined with the realisation that this assumption was not widely shared. Further, as the patriarchal model of public life was the one imported by the coloniser, a new form of public life could be postulated which differed in every respect, including in the centrality of a male hierarchy.

This is not to suggest that such attitudes pervaded the whole of the colonised society. It is also true that in a colonised society the father or husband, treated as inferior at work and in the public world where the model of maleness offered was authoritarian and often brutal, often found that the only place he could play this proscribed role was within the family, with the resulting brutalisation of his wife and children. James Connolly succinctly described the situation of working-class and colonised women as 'the slave of the slave'. It is also true that the colonial system reproduced its own codes of gender relations within large numbers of the families of the colonised, especially its middle layers, often in exaggerated form. Irish literature of the beginning of the century is rich in examples.

It would clearly be absurd to suggest that repression and abuse did not occur within the family in colonised societies, and that husbands and fathers did not abuse their power. Yet there are many instances which show that family relations in such a society could be different. The fact that the men of a colonised people did not play the role allocated by the coloniser to men in general as the rulers of the world could have the effect of democratising relations within the family, allowing it to play a role as an alternative model of human organisation to that offered by civic society. The experience of post-colonial societies has been one of widespread emigration, often of married men, which has placed greater responsibility on the shoulders of the women left behind and altered the power relationships within the family. Further, the folk memory of the family as a centre of solidarity against a hostile and invading power has given appeals to the importance of family life a greater resonance in countries with such an experience than they have in colonising and imperialist countries, where there is little contradiction between the family and the civic power.

Anne Devlin

We first find an illustration of intra-familial democracy, an assumption of equality with men, in the autobiography of Robert Emmet's housekeeper and political confidante, Anne Devlin, as told to Brother Luke Cullen of the Carmelite Monastery, Glasnevin.

Significantly, Brother Cullen begins his account with an introduction to Anne Devlin's family which established her genealogy as the daughter of two families which were rebels in the Wicklow area for several generations. Her cousins were prominent members of the United Irishmen, and one of them was later arrested with Emmet.

Because of his family connections, Anne Devlin's father, along with two of her uncles and two cousins, was arrested during the 1798 Uprising and held in prison for two years. Food had to be brought to him, and this task fell to her 'because I could sit a horse and manage him with more skill than she [her sister] could.'[13]

The model of shrinking femininity later propounded by the Catholic church as appropriate for Irish womanhood was clearly one not thought of by Anne Devlin and her friends. In the carnage of the Uprising death came often, and respect for the fallen rebels was a further site of resistance. Two young United Irishmen were buried in the Glen of Imaal.

> The people said that men so faithful in life should, if possible, be laid together in death.
>
> Dwyer's two sisters immediately took up the notion to have McAlister and Magee disinterred and brought to Kilranagh and laid in the same grave with their faithful comrades. I joined these ardent young women in their plan for the exhumation. We spoke to some young men, carpenters, to make coffins which work was soon done.
>
> And on the Saturday night following, we, with other young women volunteers, set out with a horse and dray, for no man dare venture on so perilous a mission without risk of being shot. . . .
>
> [Later when] the day arrived for placing the garlands on the graves of the fallen brave, the young women of the place assembled and the procession moved off, led by my cousins, each person dressed in white. The rear was brought up by some fearless young men, while the more cautious and sedate availed themselves of some advantageous position to view in silence and unseen the little pageant as it moved along.[14]

It was hardly surprising therefore, that when Robert Emmet wanted someone he could trust to keep his house he chose Anne Devlin, who was recommended to him by her cousin Arthur Devlin, a fellow conspirator. She makes clear the basis of their relationship: 'it is a great mistake to say that I was a hired servant. I did not, nor did my father, or mother, in any way stipulate wages. . . . Such a thought was never entertained by me or one of my family.'[15]

When the rebellion failed Anne Devlin was arrested and subjected to a mock hanging in an attempt to make her reveal Emmet's whereabouts. There followed two and a half years in jail, during which she was subjected to extraordinary ill-treatment, which broke her health. Her young brother, James, arrested like most of her family, died of his ill-treatment at the age of ten. Anne proudly points out that at Christmas 1803 no fewer than twenty-one members of her extended family were in jail for suspected involvement in the rebellion.

The catalogue of her ill-treatment makes dismal reading, yet it is interpolated throughout with her defiant statements asserting her moral and spiritual superiority to her tormentors (all men), and her appreciation of the kindness of the wife of one of the warders. She died of poverty and ill-health in 1851, at the age of seventy.

I have dwelt on the story of Anne Devlin (which forms the basis for Pat Murphy's 1983 award-winning film of the same name) for two reasons. Firstly, the true story is in more marked contrast than usual to that learned from the official history of the formation of the Irish state, in which Anne Devlin is perfunctorily dismissed as 'Robert Emmet's housekeeper' who did not betray him, and the attention is focused on his fiancée, Sarah Curran, who suffered scarcely at all from the association and later married someone else. She was the subject of a Thomas Moore nationalist ballad, but Anne Devlin was not. Secondly, Anne Devlin's story shows the profundity of the roots of nationalism in family tradition, the manner in which it is transmitted through families, and the extent to which it obliterates distinctions between the roles of men and women.

GENDER CONFUSION AS A POLITICAL WEAPON

We find a different form of the obliteration of this distinction in accounts of the activities of the secret agrarian societies which flourished in the first half of the nineteenth century. As well as pressing the immediate economic demands of those they represented, they were linked with a variety of peasant rituals and customs, using and transforming them into political idiom.

The most conspicuous evidence of the cross-over with other forms of peasant custom such as Mummers and Strawboys was the symbolic dress of male insurgents, and in particular the systematic adoption of female clothing: bonnets, gowns and petticoats were pressed into service in transgressive costume drama . . . the assumption of a female persona was taken to the point where some of the Whiteboy organizations ('whiteboy' itself signifies the wearing of a white smock) masqueraded under female soubriquets: the Lady Clare boys, Lady Rock, Terry Alt's mother and, in the nineteenth century, the Molly Maguires from the west of Ireland who later resurfaced as a militant organization in the coalfields of Pennsylvania in the 1870s.[16]

Women were heavily involved in popular movements for social change throughout the nineteenth century, especially in the widespread agrarian agitation of that time. In 1833, during the tithe wars, two tithe proctors were murdered by stoning in County Cork by a group which included a number of women, and in 1843 Bridget Maher was arrested and tried for trying to burn down the house of one Thomas Coughlan as part of a Ribbon conspiracy.[17]

Women-only mobs, or mobs led by women, made their appearance around the time of the famine, and they were frequently involved in election riots. 'What is interesting is that these societies appear to have been unconcerned with gender differences . . . Such activity was communal activity, for the benefit of all. There is no political consciousness of difference between men and women.'[18] This came later, in the 1880s, when women began to assert themselves as women, usually claiming a moral superiority over men. This arose from the influence of the emerging women's movement in Britain, which emphasised the superior moral qualities of women, an idea not prevalent, for example, in the German women's movement, which owed its genesis more directly to the labour movement and saw women as partners in that struggle.

WOMEN AND THE FENIANS

The specific circumstances of the nationalist struggle in Ireland in the late eighteenth and nineteenth centuries sometimes forced women to play a leading role, and often an independent one, while they did not identify their objectives as different from that of the movement as a whole.

The first women's political movement was the Ladies' Committee, founded in October 1865, mainly by wives or relatives of Fenian leaders, soon after the first trials of Fenians began. Mary Jane O'Donovan Rossa, Letitia Luby and the sisters of John O'Leary, Ellen and Mary, were among its most prominent members. The main task it set itself was raising money to support the families of those imprisoned, and it continued its work for six years.[19]

But Fenian women did not restrict themselves to fundraising. Although some Fenian leaders showed themselves susceptible to the prevailing Victorian notions of appropriate behaviour for women, these views were contested by others and by some of the women themselves.

Police records show that women were active in the smuggling of literature and arms into Ireland. In February 1866 a Catherine Tracey was brought up and charged with involvement in the making of pikes and pike staves; in May 1878 a Mrs Carroll, who dealt in American beef, was accused of importing rifles with the beef, while a variety of arms was found under her bed when her house was searched. In October 1865 a Fenian informer reported to Charles E. K. Kortright, the British Consul in Philadelphia: 'several thousand women have gone home bearing on their persons parts of rifles or revolvers . . .'. Even allowing that he exaggerated to enhance his own importance, this is unlikely to have been totally fabricated.[20]

There are numerous reports of women being dismissed from their jobs as schoolteachers for their political opinions. However, the single most important group of women to support the Fenians were the Irish servant girls in America. There a 'Fenian Sisterhood' was formed, and had three hundred circles throughout the US, mainly involved in fund-raising activities.[21]

Mary Jane O'Donovan Rossa was the most consistent campaigner for the Fenians. The daughter of a rebel family and the author of nationalist poetry, she met Jeremiah O'Donovan Rossa, already twice widowed, shortly after she left school. Within a year of their marriage O'Donovan Rossa was arrested and sentenced to penal servitude for life.

Mary Jane toured America to raise support for the cause, giving poetry readings and meeting political leaders, including the US President, General Grant. After her husband's release and exile to America she co-edited with him the newspaper *The United Irishman*, and often stood in for him when ill-health made him unable to carry out political engagements. She continued writing nationalist poetry until her death in 1916.

Margaret Ward has described how the Ladies' Land League pursued the campaign against evictions when the leaders of the Land League were in prison, and pursued a more radical agenda than the men, ultimately quarrelling bitterly with them over strategy, with Anna Parnell breaking decisively with her brother Charles because of his opposition to their more radical programme.[22]

Tom Clarke was the only Fenian to also play an active role in the 1916 Rising, and he was a signatory to the Proclamation. His wife, Kathleen, was an active participant in the Rising and War of Independence, and her subsequent experiences within the new Irish state clearly illustrate the treatment of women by the nationalist movement once it was distilled into a party and had taken political power in the new state.

Again, she came from a family of revolutionaries, and her uncle, John Daly, was arrested as a Fenian and jailed in England on her sixth birthday, where he befriended Tom Clarke and many years later introduced him to his niece. Her description of the attitude of his mother, her grandmother, is a telling account of the transmission of political belief within families: 'Poor grandmother, he was her favourite son, suffering through love of his country, a love she had instilled in him. She was a grand woman, whose sorrow for her son's suffering was deep, but whose pride in the fact that he could suffer and, if necessary, die for Ireland's freedom was greater.'[23]

She gives a graphic illustration of the relationship between nationalism and religion, and the priorities instilled in the family, in her account of the grandmother's prayers: 'She was a very devout Catholic, and took great pleasure in teaching us our prayers. . . . The first was always for Ireland's freedom, and when Uncle John was imprisoned the second was for his release. Then we prayed for all the relations alive and dead, ending up with "God make a good child of me".'[24]

Although the family was middle class, the constant danger of arrest for the men made it imperative for the women to be able to earn a living, so she was apprenticed to a dressmaker and at the age of eighteen set up her own dressmaking business.

Kathleen Clarke was a founding member of Cumann na mBan. She was selected to take charge of the Irish Republican Brotherhood if the whole Supreme Council was arrested. She was arrested after the Rising and execution of the leaders, including her husband, and imprisoned in England with Constance Markievicz and Maud Gonne. She opposed the Treaty, and found herself increasingly isolated within Sinn Féin. Although she disliked de Valéra, she was a founding member of Fianna Fáil.

Her relations with de Valéra were strained. Asked not to run for the Senate because this would have meant there would be two women candidates, she remarks: 'I got the impression that I was being tested to find out if I was the pliable type de Valéra seemed so fond of gathering round him. Well, I was not. I was not ready to acquiesce in things which I considered wrong, which was unfortunate for my success in public life.'[25]

This comment sums up the fate of many women who had been trained by their family, background and political activity 'not to acquiesce in things [they] considered wrong', and were now confronted with many of these things dressed up in new forms after formal political independence was won.[26]

3. WOMEN AND THE FOUNDATION OF THE STATE

Given the oppressively masculine nature of the colonial state which ruled Ireland (as well as Britain itself and the other colonies in the British Empire), it was perhaps inevitable that women would play a major role in the struggle to overthrow it, and that the battle of women for the vote and other rights gave strength and depth to the nationalist enterprise. While much is now being written about the organisation of women during the early part of the century, a lot of the discussion concerns the extent to which 'national' demands and concerns were allowed to override those of women, or the manner in which women sought to maintain their independence from the nationalist movement.

However, such an approach risks subordinating actual historical processes to the preoccupations of today, where the debate about separate organisation is a central one in the feminist movement. It is also based on acceptance of the modern propaganda of the Irish state, which projects the present domination of a conservative, patriarchal, Catholic, pro-capitalist outlook back onto the nationalist movement, implying a hegemony for this element which was not there.[27]

A number of emancipatory movements, cultural, women's, labour and national, were intertwined in the movement which led to 1916 and the War of Independence. These were not distinct, separate movements, but part of a generalised eruption of resistance to the *status quo*, and most of the leading personalities were involved in more than one area. For example, playwright Sean O'Casey was a leading member of the Irish Transport and General Workers' Union and of the Irish Citizen Army, and was active in the Gaelic League, before becoming involved as a writer with the Abbey Theatre; Constance Markievicz was involved in the labour and women's movement as well as the nationalist movement; Maud Gonne was closely associated with women like Hanna Sheehy-Skeffington and the labour movement through James Connolly; the great Abbey actress Sarah Allgood was a member of Inghinidhe na hÉireann, as William Butler Yeats was a member of the Irish Republican Brotherhood.

These few examples give no real flavour of the multi-faceted activity of the time, in which thousands of people were involved in a variety of inter-penetrating organisations and committees, favouring one over another according to the needs of the moment. One participant described the atmosphere among young people of both sexes at the time: 'Many a young man and woman grew up dreaming of dying for Ireland and leaving behind a name immortal in the country's memory. . . . But in our day, under the new leadership, young people began to think that living for the country and doing something for it might be as good as dying for it.'[28]

What is clear is that women were involved in all of these organisations. The Gaelic League was the first association to admit men and women on equal terms, and many women joined. Lady Gregory was one of the founders of the Abbey Theatre, and arguably the person most essential to its survival and success. Thousands of women flocked to join Inghinidhe na hÉireann (Daughters of Ireland) and later Cumann na mBan (the Woman's Association), as well as the Irish Women's Franchise League; the Irish Citizen Army was open to both men and women and, according to Constance Markievicz, hundreds of women joined and participated fully in all its activities, including military manoeuvres: 'They took part in all marches, and even in the manoeuvres that lasted all night. Moreover, Connolly made it quite clear to us that unless we took our share in the drudgery of training and preparing, we should not be allowed to take any share at all in the fight. You may judge how fit we were, when I tell you that sixteen miles was the length of our last route march.'[29] Dr Kathleen Lynn was the medical officer of the ICA, with the rank of Captain.

This is not to say that the male leaders of the nationalist movement were unequivocal in their support for the equal participation and rights of women. Some, like James Connolly, were, while others were definitely not. Eoin McNéill, for example, at the meeting on 25 November 1913 which launched the Volunteers said in his presidential address: 'There will be work to do for large numbers who could not be in the marching line. There would be work for the women.'[30] According to Kathleen Clarke, one of the seven signatories to the 1916 Proclamation opposed the inclusion in it of the equal appeal to Irish women, but she refused to reveal which one, except to state that it was not her husband Tom.[31]

What is important to note is the extent to which the women were, on the whole, more radical and more socially concerned than at least some of the men. Mary Colum's observation is relevant here: 'Except for Mrs [Stopford] Green . . . none of our other women guests had any personal ambition that I ever could discover. . . . One quality was common to all of them – they would work for their country without counting the cost.

'Few of the men has as rich personalities as the women.'[32]

Differing aspirations

There clearly were differences between the conception of national freedom and independence held by many of the male leaders, and the preoccupations of the women involved in the movement. Given the patriarchal nature of the British state (and all states), for many men who had never challenged the economic and social fundamentals on which it rested the question of independence was posited in terms of replacing that state with an Irish replica of it. These men were mainly preoccupied with constitutional issues, with state-formation and international legitimacy, with creating an alternative, but parallel, government to that exercised from London. While Pearse, Connolly, McDonagh and others were concerned with the social and cultural content of the new society they hoped to create, many of the others were more interested in the outward signs of independence, a point already noted by Connolly.

Women were already excluded from the state emanating from London, so any replica of the British state would equally fail to allow them to play their full role in public life. The questions with which they concerned themselves, apart from the issue of the vote, were those of the welfare of the community, especially of women and children. These women were deeply involved in the anti-conscription campaign, in supporting the labour movement, especially during the 1913 Lockout, and were engaged in welfare work, organising food distribution and children's outings, throughout that period. They were also involved in the temperance movement and in campaigning against 'morality' legislation which seemed to place the blame for prostitution on the shoulders of women.[33] In later years, reflecting on what had become of her erstwhile comrades, Kathleen Clarke summed up the difference between men and women in politics, in her eyes: 'It is extraordinary the change that comes over men, or most men, when they get a little taste of power; they seem to become so intolerant.'[34]

Constance Markievicz always felt that the interests of women and of the poor were intimately linked, and that once the question of formal independence was settled then they could come into their own. 'I have no difficulty in imagining a time when the two great world problems of woman and labour shall fuse into one ... when the (political) shouting and the tumult has died down the two world forces of feminism and labour will again emerge and dominate the situation.'[35] In her later years, when she had tasted the by now somewhat bitter fruits of political independence, she referred positively to the decentralised nature of Irish society under colonisation, and saw in this hope for the future.[36]

What actually came into being with Independence, following the Treaty, was a highly centralised state, modelled in every significant way on its colonial predecessor. Ashis Nandy has described, in the context of India, the extent to which the culture of colonialism was based on patriarchal stereotypes: 'Western sexual stereotypes ... produced a cultural consensus in which political and socio-economic dominance symbolised the dominance of men and masculinity over women and feminity.'[37] Such political and socio-economic dominance of one group over another was reproduced by the new rulers of Ireland, and replicated in the state they formed. Nandy's observation of the effect this had on British society also has relevance for Ireland both before and after Independence: 'It de-emphasized speculation, intellection and caritas as feminine, and justified a limited cultural role for women – and femininity – by holding that the softer side of human nature was irrelevant to the public sphere.'[38]

The two-house parliamentary system, the legal system, the structure, and, to a large extent, the composition, of the civil service, remained largely unchanged after Independence. In 1922 21,000 of the civil servants were former British civil servants, with only 131 having served under Dáil Éireann.[39] Perhaps because they were only too well aware of the dangers of allowing any power and initiative to stray outside the administrative centre, the new rulers of Ireland imposed a rigidly centralised regime, even standardising what had not been standardised before, like the Irish language. Thus today, with a population running to only three and a half million, less than that of many large cities, the Irish state is one of the most highly-centralised in Western Europe.

Only in one important respect did the founders of the new state depart from their British model: in the adoption of a written Constitution, spelling out the rights of citizens. At the outset, in 1921, this gave the vote and equal civil rights to all adult women, thus granting to women in the Free State the vote seven years earlier than some of their sisters in the North, who obtained it under the later British legislation (the earlier 1918 legislation restricted the vote to women over thirty). It is significant that it has been the Constitution, and not any of the other institutions of the state, which has been the battleground for defending and expanding the rights of women since.

The split in Sinn Féin over the Treaty divided politically active women, although all six women deputies in the Dáil opposed the Treaty, and Cumann na mBan as a whole rejected it. A new women's organisation was set up to support the Treaty side, composed almost entirely of wives and other relatives of men who were pro-Treaty, including, according to Margaret Ward, women who had not before been active in politics, like the wife of Arthur Griffith. The fact that the pro-Treaty side was less than positive about proposals to give the vote to all women over twenty-one ensured that many women more prominent in the suffrage than in the nationalist movement, like Hanna Sheehy Skeffington, also opposed the Treaty.[40]

In retrospect, the opposition of the majority of politically-active women to the Treaty can be seen as the first step towards their gradual exclusion from public life in the new Ireland. In the atomisation of the movement which followed, some fell out of active politics altogether, some threw their lot in with the Labour Party, others with Sinn Féin after the foundation of Fianna Fail by de Valéra in 1926, while others, like Kathleen Clarke, went with Fianna Fail, at least for the time being. She and Jenny Wyse-Power, veteran of the Ladies' Land League, the Gaelic League, Sinn Féin and Cumann na mBan, were the only two women senators to consistently raise their voices for women's equality within the corridors of power.[41]

THE NEW STATE

The Cumann na nGaedhael government which came to power in the new Irish state introduced a number of legislative measures that further restricted the rights of women and modified the statements of equality contained in the 1916 Proclamation and the 1922 Constitution. These included discriminatory legislation relating to illegitimacy and divorce, the barring of women from jury service (a right they had under the previous British legislation), measures to restrict women's access to employment and equal treatment at work, both in the civil service and in industry, and laws relating to issues like contraception which bore especially heavily on women. The main voice raised against them in the Oireachtas was that of Jenny Wyse-Power, often supported by Kathleen Clarke. The Labour Party actually supported legislation which discriminated against women at work.[42]

Fianna Fail, despite its rhetoric, bore little resemblance to the broad-based nationalist movement, with all its political, social and cultural diversity, that had brought such women into public life. It was a thoroughly patriarchal organisation, and de Valéra was person-ally hostile to women's equality. And although it was born of a split with Cumann na nGaedhael, that split had more to do with form than substance, as the formula devised by de Valéra for eventual entry into the Dáil showed. While Fianna Fail appealed to a more radical section of the electorate than did Cumann na nGaedhael, and instituted a programme of social reform when it came to power, it had no differences with its predecessor on the fundamental nature and institutions of the state and its relationship with its former masters.

As Kathleen Clarke caustically remarked on Fianna Fail's accession to power:

> a change took place. Things which they had condemned as wrong for W. T. Cosgrave's government to do became right for them. I had understood (perhaps foolishly) that the things which they, as the opposition, claimed were wrong would remain wrong. . . .
>
> Partition and the Irish language were the first two things they were going to tackle when they became the government, but nothing was being done about either.[43]

THE 1937 CONSTITUTION

Having taken control of the new state in 1932, Fianna Fail set about legitimising it by writing its own Constitution for it, replacing the more radical one of 1921.[44] The 'national aims' of ending the partition of the country and restoring the Irish language were given aspirational status, while the real work of consolidating the conservative nature of the institutions of the new state went ahead. A central part of this was the subordinate role assigned to women, whose role was to be circumscribed by their redefinition as 'mothers', and limited by a Constitutional insistence on 'their *duties* in the home' (my emphasis).[45]

This was opposed by many of the female veterans of the nationalist movement, and Hanna Sheehy Skeffington organised a public campaign against it. The campaign was supported by Kathleen Clarke, among others, causing her to be expelled from her cumann of Fianna Fail. All the women's organisations (except Cumann na mBan, which, like other republican organisations, stood aloof from the debate on the grounds that they did not recognise the state anyway) opposed it, but de Valéra was adamant that the father was the natural breadwinner of the family, and that women should be bound by their duties within the home. The Constitution was narrowly voted into existence, with thirty-one per cent of the electorate abstaining.

Article 41 of the Constitution, recognising the support given to the state by women 'by her life within the home' and seeking to ensure that she would not have to neglect her 'duties' there by going out to work, underpinned discriminatory measures against women, like the ban on married women working in the public service and a raft of discriminatory regulations in the social welfare area. The ban on women working in the civil service paralleled a similar British regulation which was in force there until the 1960s.

Both the letter of the Constitution, the accompanying legislation and the spirit it embodied, militated heavily against the involvement of women in public life, and by the end of the Second World War most of those women who had devoted decades of their lives to the creation of a different society and political system in Ireland had virtually disappeared. Some, like Constance Markievicz, were dead. Others, like those who ran on an Independent ticket in the 1943 election, stressing the needs of women, were defeated and drifted out of politics. The eventual resignation of Kathleen Clarke from Fianna Fail was symbolical: 'I was sorry to have to do so. I liked public life, and liked having a say in the affairs of my country, and felt I had earned a right to do so, but the qualities which made for success in the war for independence were no longer needed.'[46]

Women might have had a place in the revolution, but for Ireland's new rulers, aping their imperial masters in this as in so many things, they certainly had no place in government. The position of women in Irish society thus worsened in the new state, because the political activities previously available to them in the nationalist movement were now closed off, except for the few women who remained active in the labour movement (Helena Maloney and Nora Connolly O'Brien being among the most important). This movement, however, was quickly domesticated and adapted itself to the requirements of the new political élite.

With the transformation of the nationalist movement into two broadly similar political parties, both intent on taking over and running the state they had inherited from the British virtually intact, women's access to politics was closed off and they were driven into the domestic sphere to an extent which had not existed before, under the British administration. Then the domination of a colonial power had created a socially broad and varied oppositional response, with space in it for women. This space disappeared when that oppositional movement developed into the parties which now competed for, and alternated in, power within that state.

4. FINDING A ROLE OUTSIDE THE STRUCTURES OF THE STATE

This period may have marked the end of one era for women in Ireland, but it did not mark the end of their activity in society. Faced with the reactionary, patriarchal society independent Ireland had become, they had to adopt new strategies more appropriate to the time they were living in. Their old talents for organisation around questions of immediate interest to women, children and the poor came to the fore, though in a more muted way than in the early years of the century, when Maud Gonne and Inghinidhne na hÉireann, and the women around Connolly, devoted much of their energies to raising money to feed the children of the urban poor.

THE IRISH HOUSEWIVES' ASSOCIATION

In 1941 a group of young women, all Protestant and in their twenties and early thirties, started a petition seeking the amelioration of the conditions of the poor and unemployed, with particular reference to control over the distribution and pricing of food. They obtained 640 signatures and had forty at the first meeting. They set up the Irish Housewives' Association, later linking up with other women's organisations of different social origin, like the Irish Women Workers' Union, in pursuit of price control, proper rationing, school meals and salvaging waste. They were joined by a number of veterans of the suffrage movement.

In her account of the history of the IHA Tweedy acknowledges that at the outset the majority of the membership was Protestant.[47] Outside the north-east corner of the country the early movement for national and cultural freedom and for social reform had also contained a high proportion of Protestant women. In the north-east, while a women's franchise movement existed in Belfast and other northern towns, involving mainly Protestant women, they were suspicious of the links between their sisters in the south and nationalism. They all came together in a Women's Convention on the Home Rule Bill (which contained no reference to women's suffrage) in 1912, but parted on the national question.

The fact that Edward Carson refused to take up the issue of women's suffrage not only made clear the links between an imperialist ideology and patriarchy, but also left Unionist women with nowhere to go without breaking with Unionism.[48] That few of them were prepared to do so is illustrated by the fact that 234,046 voted for a women's equivalent of the Ulster Covenant, despite the subordinate role in which they were cast.[49] The weakness of feminism among Northern Protestant women today is the legacy of that heritage.

However, the fact remains that in the rest of Ireland large numbers of women from Protestant backgrounds flocked to the ranks of the broadly nationalist movement in Ireland. When one considers the alternatives available to them – constricted lives within the framework of the dreary social round of the social caste into which they had been born, wilful ignorance of the lives of the majority of the people around them, an extremely restricted outlet for any cultural aspirations they might have – it is hardly surprising that the adventurous and intelligent among them seized the opportunity to throw off the restrictions imposed on them by birth and sex and sought to forge a new society in which they could play a full part.

The names of Constance Markievicz, Maud Gonne, Charlotte Despard are well known, but there are many other lesser-known figures who found it easy to break the allegiance expected of them to the imperial power, and maintained by their male relatives. One example is the Honourable Albinia Broderick, sister of the Earl of Midleton who was the leader of the southern Unionists. She changed her name to Gobnait de Bruadair and built a hospital in County Kerry in restitution for her family's expropriation of land. In 1922 she was elected on to Kerry County Council as a member of Sinn Féin and became one of the party's most intransigent republicans.[50] Charlotte Despard's brother was Lord French, Viceroy of Ireland and responsible for martial law and the Black and Tans, another example of the difference between the attitudes of the male and female members of such families.[51]

This Protestant female dissenting tradition continued after Independence, when the male members of the Protestant community who remained in Ireland settled down to maintaining their economic positions in finance, commerce, industry and the professions left untouched by the new regime. While the men on the whole remained politically mute, failing to oppose even measures which discriminated against their community, the women's organisations which survived, or were formed in, the new state owed a debt to women from this small Protestant community, and their involvement also helped ensure that these organisations escaped the Catholic confessionalism which dominated so many social movements at that time. These organisations became a rare meeting ground for women from different social and religious backgrounds who were able to discuss issues of concern to all women in an environment free from religious and political supervision.

The Irish Housewives' Association was made up of energetic young women barred from the world of work and of politics by the prevailing ethos of the time. As Hilda Tweedy remarks: 'It was unusual for women to work outside the home and quite difficult for them to find jobs.'[52] Some, like Moira Corcoran in Drogheda, were women forced to resign from the civil service on marriage, and who found their 'duties in the home' an inadequate outlet for their energies. However, they had an impact on government policy and succeeded in having food rationed on a fair basis during and after the war, in restricting price rises and in having milk pasteurised. They also campaigned, with the Irish Women Workers' Union, for improvement in the conditions of women working in domestic service, of whom there were still considerable numbers, and supported the successful laundry workers' strike in 1945.

In her foreword to Tweedy's book Margaret McCurtain points out: 'Conscious of the dual role of women in the mid-century they presented to the public the solid frontage of the Irish housewife; strategically they instructed their members on how to negotiate the complex maze of the Irish party machine.'[53]

THE IRISH COUNTRYWOMEN'S ASSOCIATION

The Irish Countrywomen's Association played a similar role for women in rural Ireland. Founded in 1910 as the United Irishwomen, and linked to the cooperative movement, its objectives were: 'So far as women's knowledge and influence will avail, they will strive for a higher standard of material comfort and physical well-being in the country home, a more advanced agricultural economy, and a social existence a little more in harmony with the intellect and temperament of our people.'[54]

Like the cooperative movement, the United Irishwomen was part of the broader movement of national awakening which swept the country at the beginning of the century, of which the establishment of an independent state was only one, and, for some, not the foremost, objective. Making a remarkably modern criticism of the female image of Ireland current in nationalist circles at the time of the foundation of the United Irishwomen, Horace Plunkett wrote:

> That Ireland, more than any country, is spoken of as a woman is probably due to the appearance in our national affairs of qualities which men call womanly. And this impression is not merely the cheap attribution of racial inferiority by the alien critic with which we are familiar, it is our feeling about ourselves. The Dark Rosaleen, straining her tear-dimmed eyes for foreign aid, is an image of man's creation. I have often wondered how we should fare if the shrewd practical sense, the housekeeperly instinct – real womanly qualities of the greatest value to the modern state – had freer play in our public life. I write of women's work, not women's votes, for we who join in this book treat of things which neither parliaments nor governments can do for a people – things which they must do for themselves. But it is quite as true than in the sphere of voluntary effort as in that of legislation and administration that no country needs woman's help more than our own at the present time, or gets it less. If all this were changed, more might be done in Ireland for Ireland.[55]

The organisation emphasised the importance of providing a vibrant social life in the countryside as a bulwark against emigration. '. . . the starved soul of womanhood is crying out over the world for an intellectual life and for more chance of earning a living', wrote one of its founders, Ellice Pilkington. 'If Ireland will not listen to this cry, its daughters will go on slipping silently away to other countries, as they have been doing – all the best of them, all the bravest, all those most mentally alive, all those who would have made the best wives and mothers – and they will leave at home the timid, the stupid and the dull to help in the deterioration of the race to breed sons as sluggish as themselves.'[56]

The United Irishwomen and its successor, the ICA, failed to stem the flood of emigration, but it did improve the quality of rural life for tens of thousands of Irish women. According to Kathleen Delap, who along with her sisters joined in the 1940s, it successfully fought for a proper advisory service for women on farms (one was already provided, in the form of agricultural advisors, for men), for piped water to all homes, for the widespread use of electricity in the home. The water scheme ran into opposition from the Irish Farmers Association, she said, on the basis that 'they had sunk wells. Why should others get it for free? And why should they (the farmers) have to pay higher rates for it?'[57]

Perhaps the main contribution the ICA made to the lives of thousands of women was the opportunity it gave for them to leave their homes and engage in social activity with other women. Much of this was educational, the teaching of a wide range of skills and crafts ranging from the traditional female skills of cooking and sewing to less traditional ones like carpentry. The ICA centre at An Grianán in County Louth, presented and maintained by the Kellogg Foundation, offered an opportunity to get away from home and family for a week or two to develop skills and, equally importantly, to build friendships and exchange ideas. Many of the women who were forces for change in their local community – town-dwellers as well as countrywomen, teachers and nurses as well as farmers' wives – were graduates of An Grianán.

The 1937 Constitution sought to imprison women in the family, and to subordinate their role to that of their 'duties in the home'. The Irish Countrywomen's Association and the Irish Housewives' Association sought to expand and develop their role in the family so that it influenced society as a whole. As such they were virtually unassailable by the patriarchal institutions which otherwise excluded women from public life. They offered women an avenue through which to fight for a better life for themselves and their children and a voice in the development of public policy.

As the modern feminist movement developed in the 1970s, largely under the influence of the US women's movement, the ICA and the IHA were seen as conservative and were pushed into the background. Certainly the fact that they unquestioningly supported the institution of the family brought them into conflict with younger feminists. Nonetheless, the IHA was instrumental in forming the Council for the Status of Women and the establishment of the Commission on the Status of Women. It eventually dissolved, feeling its work was now being done by other organisations. The ICA continued to plough its own furrow, attracting almost 30,000 members in the 1970s, a figure which rests at 23,000 today.

Such was the image of the ICA that much surprise was expressed when the ICA took a poll of its members in 1992 on the subject of abortion, and came up with a majority supporting abortion in circumstances of rape, incest and threat to the health of the mother. But this should not have been such a surprise. In 1972 the organisation was due to attend an international conference where it would be expected to vote on family planning. Contraception was illegal in Ireland, and would be for another seven years, though the first Commission on the Status of Women had recommended access to family planning. The membership of the ICA was asked to read its recommendation and send in its views. 'A good majority sent in replies saying they were in favour', according to Kathleen Delap. 'We would get a general consensus on things. I can remember that particular one in 1972. We had always been on good terms with the local papers, and the *Donegal Democrat* wrote a furious letter saying it would have nothing to do with the ICA again.'[58]

The ICA, like the IHA, was formed as an interdenominational and non-party political organisation, and indeed was dominated by women from Protestant and Anglo-Irish backgrounds for the first years of its existence, though this had changed by the 1960s. This helped in ensuring that no particular religious or political ethos dominated, which was rarely the case with male-dominated organisations in this period, when even trade unions, for example, held masses to mark the opening of their conferences into the 1970s, and a Catholic ethos dominated the GAA and even formerly non-denominational organisations like the Gaelic League. However, the Gaelic game of camogie, played by women, was an exception to this. It was opposed by luminaries of the Catholic church like Archbishop McQuaid on the grounds of indecency, but widely played by young, mainly Catholic, women, nonetheless.

One is tempted to conclude that, being organisations for mere women, the ICA and IHA were not thought worth dominating by the male hierarchies which so thoroughly occupied political and economic life. Furthermore, their objectives were different – they sought changes in society, albeit often small ones, not positions within the male-dominated political hierarchies.

'We encouraged women to go into politics, but not as ICA', said Kathleen Delap. Echoing Kathleen Clarke, she added: 'I don't think women are ambitious for themselves. They want things done, but they don't particularly want the honour and glory for themselves. A lot of us were perfectly happy bringing up families and doing other things on the side, so to speak.'[59]

Of course, these organisations still represented a minority of women, though quite a large one, and by the 1960s they had become rather tame and respectable. Kathleen Delap admits that the women who held positions on the executive had to be quite comfortably off, as they paid their own expenses to come to Dublin for meetings, and the modest membership fees might have been beyond the resources of some women.

It is erroneous to assume, however, that the women who remained outside any organisation were passive recipients of the institutional oppression which undoubtedly surrounded them, incapable of showing initiative or exerting any control over their lives and environment. The feminist movement which began in the early 1970s saw the preceding decades as years of unrelieved gloom for women in Ireland. Preoccupied with the agenda of Anglo-American feminism with its emphasis on freedom from oppressive family ties and responsibilities, equal rights at work and sexual satisfaction, it saw the lives lived by women in Ireland up to then from the standpoint of the stereotypes of middle-class suburban life which featured in feminist literature, with the added ingredient in Ireland of repressive Catholic attitudes towards sexuality.

EDUCATION, WORK AND SURVIVAL

There is no denying the secondary status accorded to women in the Republic of Ireland almost from the foundation of the state. Nor can the misogyny of the Catholic church be gainsaid. On top of that, the thousands of Irish women who participated in the events which led to the foundation of the state were, literally, written out of its history, and everything possible was done by official society to kill the tradition they represented.

But women continued to find ways to resist, and that tradition of strength and self-reliance lived on, sometimes in unlikely sur-roundings. Not only in organisations like the ICA and the IHA, but within families and local communities, women found ways to survive and assert themselves, even if not in the terms taken up by their daughters and grand-daughters in the 1970s. And, while excluded from playing a full role in economic life, women did obtain equal access to education, at least up to second level (only a small minority of the population got to third level before the 1970s).

In 1935, for instance, 3,269 boys and 2,534 girls took the Intermediate Certificate examination and 1,325 boys and 840 girls took the Leaving Certificate examination. Twenty years later this discrepancy had virtually disappeared, with more girls than boys taking the Intermediate Certificate (6,634 girls as against 5,677 boys). For the Leaving Certificate the figures were almost level, 3,153 boys as against 2,945 girls.

By 1975 girls had overtaken boys in both examinations, and the total figures had been hugely increased by the introduction of free secondary education in 1967. In 1975, 23,734 girls took the Intermediate Certificate, compared with 21,270 boys, and 15,687 took the Leaving Certificate, as against 13,519 boys.[60]

Thus while girls might have been destined for 'duties in the home' under the Constitution, for most families who could afford it this fate was combined with a recognition of the usefulness of a good education for its daughters. That education might prepare them for a narrow range of activities – predominantly office work, teaching and nursing – but a certain shrewd recognition of economic realities was combined with the Catholic pieties sustained by officialdom.

The fact that more girls than boys were taking state examinations by the end of the 1950s is also a reflection of the practice in farming families of providing for the boys with land and for the girls with education. The eligibility of girls in the marriage market was enhanced by their ability to earn and bring savings into the household, and even to work for a while after marriage, especially when this was facilitated by the presence of a grandmother in the home to look after the children. Teachers were much sought after as farmers' wives in the 1940s, 1950s and 1960s for this reason. (This did not apply to working class girls, who, like most of their brothers, were excluded from secondary education until the 1960s, and even up to today have a largely negative experience of education.)[61]

In the arranged marriages which were still common in rural Ireland up to the 1950s women were sought for their intelligence and ability to work. Women and girls were expected to work in the fields as well as do domestic work. 'Also, in areas where seasonal migration was common, women would be left in charge of a farm for months at a time while the men were absent in England or Scotland.'[62] This was also a result of emigration; when married men emigrated, as they often did, especially in the west of Ireland, the women were left in total charge of the farm, running it and rearing the family alone for years on end. The men returned on holiday two or three times a year, often the occasion for the conception of another child, but to all intents and purposes the family was a lone-parent one, headed by a woman who had to earn a living as well as run the family. The role of such women was inevitably a strong one, and provided a strong role-model for their children.

Even where the man worked at home on the farm, its financial management was often in the hands of his wife. In urban working-class families the tradition, fought for by the organised labour movement, of handing the wage-packet over to the wife who then distributed the money was still widespread. It was only in the social layer which could afford to most closely model itself on the English middle class and its Victorian heritage that the 'luxury' of a wife confined to a purely decorative and maternal role could exist. Thus the model of the economically and socially impotent urban housewife, on which so much Anglo-American feminist writing of the 1960s is based, was not one which would strike a chord with the majority of Irish women of that time.

The changes brought about in rural Ireland by greater prosperity in the 1970s did not always enhance women's role. A study by Damien Hannon and Louise Katsiaouni found 'the farmer's wife has been transformed into a housewife' by the mechanisation of agriculture and the introduction of a cash-based farmhouse budget.[63] Cows and chickens – the basis of some economic independence for farming women who sold eggs and home-made butter – had either disappeared or become the men's responsibility in more intensive production. However, 'some women maintained their involvement in the farm by taking on a new role – that of secretary and administrator.'[64]

These observations must modify Beale's contention that 'the ideology of the family functions to support male-dominated hierarchies, and is another source of continuing oppression for women. Although the idea that a woman's main role in life is to be a dedicated wife and mother was strongly challenged in the 1970s, it still has a profound influence in many areas of Irish life.'[65] In fact, Irish women stretched and expanded these categories as they elaborated survival strategies during these years, and explored avenues of controlling their lives which tended towards the subversion of the dominant ideology, even while they largely accepted its claims.

THE 1970S WOMEN'S MOVEMENT AND AFTER

Nonetheless the vision of the situation of women which inspired the Irish feminist movement which emerged in Ireland in the 1970s was one of fairly unrelieved gloom. It owed much of its inspiration to the American women's movement, as one of its founders, Mary Maher, explained. 'A couple of women came over from the US to see Máirín de Burca [a prominent woman in Sinn Féin, the radical nationalist and semi-socialist movement of the time]. A group of women came together after that, basically from two sides, the left, which had its own agenda, and frustrated urban middle-class women. It was not grafted on to any existing tradition.'[66]

This movement focused on the illegality of contraception in the Republic of Ireland, and also raised various questions of discrimination against women at work, including the forced retirement of women from the civil service on their marriage. The National Commission on the Status of Women was set up in 1970, reporting in 1972. Although regarded with suspicion by the more radical feminist movement, its recommendations included the right to family planning and the ending of discrimination against women at work.

In the women's movement tensions showed quickly between those whose concern was with the social conditions of poorer women, and those more influenced by the radical feminism which came from the US. One of the first actions of this Irish women's movement was the demonstration for contraceptive rights, involving taking a train to Belfast and back, in order to import contraceptives, then illegal in southern Ireland. 'It was meant to be a dignified demonstration of married women asserting their reproductive rights. There is a difference between reproductive rights and questions of sexuality. But some of those involved made it into something else by blowing up condoms and releasing them on the platform and all the rest of it.' said Mary Maher.[67]

The ideology of modern feminism has, quite understandably, been formed by women in the countries where it had its genesis – the United States, Britain, and the countries of Western Europe, especially in their universities. It emerged from the experience of life in the 1950s and 1960s in these countries, where post-war entrenchment forced women back into the home and increased their isolation while at the same time a general rise in the level of prosperity obviated the need for communal struggle for survival, which offered scope for useful and satisfying activity outside the home. The stultifying affect of such imprisonment in the nuclear family provided the impetus for the development of the modern women's movement.

However, the experience of the majority of women on the planet has not been that of imprisonment in the nuclear family, cut off from productive work outside the home and from communal interaction with other people, especially other women. Yet it is only in recent years that their experience has become part of the discussion within feminism.[68]

The public image of the women's movement in Ireland continues to be affected, if not dominated, by the activities of mainly young, middle-class, highly-educated urban women influenced by Anglo-American radical feminism whose concerns are those of their fellows everywhere – individual emancipation within the framework set by liberal consumerism. But the experience of this movement is that it fails to put down roots outside of this social layer, and its demands have only a limited influence on the majority of women, especially those who are poor, who are members of oppressed sub-groups, like travellers or Northern nationalists in Ireland, who experience communal oppression as well as oppression as women.

Women from poorer communities, urban and rural, have been organising in Ireland in recent years and articulating their concerns. One index of this is the number of women's groups which receive funding (albeit very limited) from the Department of Social Welfare. These amounted to 480 at the last count – almost twenty for every county in the state, and most of those involved in community work consider the real figure to be higher. Their concerns often fall outside the agenda set by liberal feminism, yet they have a deep resonance in their communities. Clearly they owe their existence to something deeper and more complex than the influence of a movement born little more than two decades ago, largely influenced by similar movements abroad. While undoubtedly influenced by the impact of feminism on the worlds of education and social work, their roots lie in deeper, and more indigenous, traditions.

5. TRADITION IN THE SERVICE OF RESISTANCE

Ireland is not the only country where, faced with a conservative lay and religious patriarchy, women found ways to use the traditions of the society to subvert that patriarchy. In so doing they often reinterpret those traditions, both secular and religious, to suit their own needs and aspirations. Here women's resistance movements are driven, not by ideology, but by the needs of the moment, and the weapons that lie to hand.

Cut off from access to public life, women develop their own strategies for challenging the *status quo*, often using quite conservative institutions to do so. Therefore women use the bits of tradition which suit them when nothing else is available. Frequently this then provides the basis for the emergence of more radical movements opposed to the *status quo*.

LATIN AMERICAN HOUSEWIVES

For example, throughout Latin America in the 1970s and 1980s women's movements founded on the role of women as housewives and mothers came to challenge the domination of military regimes. In Brazil women's community organisations took on a life of their own, organising against the rising cost of living, seeking day care and running water in the poor areas and leading eventually to the formation of a National Council on Women's Rights in 1980, a development which is remarkably similar to the role of the Irish Housewives' Association in the formation of the first Commission on the Status of Women.[69] In Argentina the project of the military dictatorship was that the family would not just be society's basic cell, but its only cell. This centrality of the family was turned against the dictatorship by the Madres de la Plaza de Mayo, founded in 1977, the mothers who demonstrated in the centre of Buenos Aires for the identification of the whereabouts of their sons and daughters who had been 'disappeared' by the military regime. In the nationalist community in Northern Ireland women who organised in support of their (mainly male) jailed relatives have played a central role in the development of community organisations.

The Argentinian example shows how the private, but universal, emotions of loss and grief played a crucial role in the awakening of a nation cowed by dictatorship, and indeed were the catalyst for the development of a movement which led eventually to its overthrow. 'These women did not try to draw up political party accords, as conventional practice dictated, but called for a new social consensus on themes that united women of different political sectors and social classes.'[70] Their success inspired others, and led to a strong housewives' protest in 1982.

In Uruguay a small, tolerant, democratic society was taken over by a military regime in the context of an economic crisis in the 1960s. In this situation 'the family retained and even reinforced its capacity as a shock absorber. It was, after all, the last bastion of warmth and security in a world turned dangerous and hostile. Home meant a stronghold where one could let aside the persona and, for a few hours, become once again the person.'[71]

The private sphere had traditionally been seen as female and the public sphere as male. But with the public sphere closed off, men were condemned to silence and political impotence. Women, how-ever, still had their private concerns, like the cost of living, though they did not immediately challenge the legitimacy of those in power. 'Theirs was an ant-like resistance, made of patience, words, gestures, and especially marked by the absence of silence. Women talked, women criticised, women protested, as they had always done, as they still do.'[72]

> The principles that guided their action were very conservative and very traditional: devoted defence of home and family at any personal cost. There was nothing 'feminist' in their formulation; motherhood and housewifery propelled them to act . . . But, more by the fact that they existed than by what they did, those women's organisations contributed to erode the monologue, the single order of discourse imposed from the top.[73]

The family here also acted as the crucible of political dissent:

In the intimacy of the private realm, mothers, aunts
and older sisters took charge of the rearing of the
younger generation and transmitted to it the
powerful, anti-regime, 'subversive' democratic values
which helped to keep the flame of hope alive. By
keeping the memory of the past alive through tales
and through their acts, they prevented the grim
authoritarian 'present' of the dictatorship from
becoming the children's reality.[74]

Thus it has been such actions of 'housewives', whether from
middle-class or impoverished families, rather than those of
ideologically-motivated feminists, which have given depth and
weight to the women's movements in these countries, and made
them into political forces to be reckoned with.

Religion has played an ambiguous role in this. While the official
church has usually supported those in power, that section of the
Catholic church which supported liberation theology and the
formation of 'basic Christian communities' has played an important
role in the organisation of women. Sometimes it has attempted to
restrict developments which challenged the teaching of the church,
notably in relation to family planning, but here it has had only
limited success.

WOMEN AND ISLAM

Although the parallels between the national struggles in Ireland and
India are striking, Ireland is often compared to Islamic society in
the role played by religious zealots in the civic life of the nation.
Such a comparison – while largely inappropriate – can be useful
when we look in some detail at the manner in which women in
Islamic societies are attempting to improve their status within the
context of their own culture.

For most Westerners the veil is the most obvious and potent symbol of the oppression of women under Islam. In the early nineteenth century many Westernised members of the élite, smarting under the criticism of their rulers, encouraged their women not to wear the veil. This often went hand-in-hand with these women obtaining a Western education, and many of them went on to put this to the service of their people.

But this impulse for change carried a price. Leila Ahmed writes: 'Colonialism's use of feminism to promote the culture of the coloniser and undermine native culture has ever since imparted to feminism in non-Western societies the taint of having served as an instrument of colonial domination, rendering it suspect in Arab eyes and vulnerable to the charge of being an ally of colonial interests. That charge has undoubtedly hindered the feminist struggle within Muslim societies.'[75]

The veil virtually disappeared in urban Egypt by the mid-twentieth century. Now, however, millions of women, especially young women, have returned to wearing some form of Islamic dress, proving that such change is not necessarily permanent. Surveys of young people in modern Egypt show that Islamic tendencies predominated among the 'new middle' class, where the parents had lower educational achievement than their children. These young people were upwardly mobile, often confronting bewildering, cosmopolitan city life for the first time, including its inequalities, consumerism and materialism. Their open attachment to Islamic values is often 'an affirmation of ethical and social customs...that those adopting the dress and affiliation (of Islam) are comfortable with and accustomed to.'[76]

The Islamic mode of dress is especially practical and important for young women from such backgrounds. It is economical, it is protective from harassment and generates respect which might not otherwise be forthcoming from strangers. It is 'a practical coping strategy, enabling women to negotiate in the new world while affirming the traditional values of their upbringing.'[77] 'In adopting Islamic dress, then, women are in effect "carving out legitimate public space for themselves" . . . The adoption of the dress does not declare women's place to be in the home, but, on the contrary, legitimises their presence outside.'[78] Indeed, Ahmed points out that women in Egypt are entering universities and the professions in unprecedented numbers.[79]

It is difficult not to share Leila Ahmed's conclusions that in countries like Egypt, where Westernised ideas were seen to have failed to deliver an uncorrupt political system, social equality or justice for the Palestinian Arabs with whom so many of the population identify, traditional beliefs are modified and moulded to suit these aspirations, and also those of women for a greatly enhanced role in public life.

The capacity of women in countries like Egypt to make advances within the framework of their culture is not to say that religious zealotry and its (usually male) leaders do not represent a great danger for women's emancipation. This danger is especially great when such zealotry is wedded to political power. But Islam is not the only world religion which contains such a danger, as the fundamentalist Jews in Israel and the many varieties of fundamentalist Christians in the United States bear witness.

CATHOLICISM

The question of the relationship of women to organised religion is an important one in Ireland because the overwhelming majority of the population practises religion, normally Catholicism. While the figures for some of the signs of religious observance have been falling over the past two decades, both successive surveys and measures of observance show a continued attachment to Catholicism. The women's movement in Ireland will not be able to advance without taking account of this.

Many aspects of Catholic traditional teaching, however, especially those relating to the role and rights of women, are challenged or rejected. Contraception is widely practised, the birth-rate outside marriage is now one of the highest in Europe and still rising, while family size has halved in the past twenty years, the Church itself champions the equal rights of women at work, men and women who leave religious life to marry are accepted and welcomed in their communities.

A little-noticed aspect of this has been the changing role of nuns, both in the Church itself and in the wider community. While the religious life offered women in the nineteenth century a socially-useful and relatively powerful role outside the confines of restricted domesticity, for a long time they accepted their subordinate role within the Church. More recently nuns have come to challenge this role within the Church, and in the broader society theirs have often been the most radical voices, criticising the partriarchal traditions of the Church and also urging it to be more involved in the concerns of the poor. Nuns have also been deeply involved in the development of locally-based women's groups, both in inner city communities and in country areas, groups which confronted issues like inequality of educational opportunity for working-class women, violence against women and reproductive rights. They have been to the fore there in urging women to assert their rights, against the 'sanctity of the family' if necessary.[80]

There are a number of reasons for this. The most obvious one is the continuing impact of Vatican II, which opened up the Church to debate on its relationship with the society in which it worked, and which allowed a wide range of dissenting views to emerge. But Sister Jo Kennedy has suggested a more specific reason why nuns in Ireland have come to play a more radical role. The development of free education for daughters of the working class in the 1950s and 1960s, through the expansion of the work of certain religious orders, meant that for the first time girls from such backgrounds could enter these orders as full sisters, rather than as the uneducated 'lay sisters', doing essentially menial work, they had been in previous decades. They brought with them a very different set of attitudes than those of the urban and rural middle class from which nuns were previously recruited.[81]

WOMEN'S GROUPS

The mushrooming of locally-based women's groups over the past few years has been the result of a marriage between the influence of modern feminism and tradition. No-one knows precisely how many there are, but one indication of their growth is given by the fact that a meeting of western women's groups with President Robinson was called in Headford, Co. Galway, in 1992 and a hall was hired for two hundred and fifty people. Over one thousand people, representing forty-two women's groups, turned up.[82] The call on the Department of Social Welfare to fund women's groups (with a small grant) grows all the time, and at the last count it came to 480, an increase of 300 on the 1990 figure.[83]

As I have argued above, the history of Ireland, especially the history of popular resistance to British rule and the social system it bolstered, created considerable opportunities for women to play a role in public life, an opportunity thousands of them seized. Economic hardships in this and the last century prompted the development of independence and resourcefulness, including emigration both of lone women and of married men, the raising by women of families alone and their development of a variety of survival strategies. The memories of these forms of resistance and survival do not disappear, they become part of a tradition, however deeply buried, and find ways of surfacing when the need arises.

6. The Development of Community-based Women's Organisations

This century saw great social and economic, as well as political, changes in Ireland, as the country became transformed from a predominantly rural to a mainly urban society, a process completed by the 1960s. This affected women in various ways. Growing prosperity reduced the drudgery which was the lot of many – but, paradoxically, it also reduced the participation of women in agricultural economic life, as agriculture became more intensive and mechanised, and women's contribution to the family economy became less important. The fall in emigration in the 1960s and 1970s, while removing a source of social dislocation and decay, reduced the number of rural women running farms and families alone. Industrial development brought more and more people into the cities and towns, which, combined with growing prosperity and the decline in domestic service and work in traditional female employments like laundries, meant that more and more women remained at home as housewives.

In the cities the old forms of community organisation broke down with the breakdown of traditional community life, centred on the extended family. Outside the major urban centres the ICA declined and the growing reliance on television for entertainment, the greater mobility of women as prosperity increased, and the reduced importance of parish activities also eroded communally-based activities. The recent growth of organised women's groups can be seen partially as a response to this.

However, it also reflects a different perception of the role of women in society. The development of the women's movement in the 1970s had a particular effect in the universities and in the media in the 1980s, and focused attention on women and their specific interests and problems. Those coming out of universities as teachers and social workers, and sometimes as trade union activists in white collar unions, had a different attitude to the role of women. They saw more problems than did their predecessors.

This coincided with changes in the position of women, especially in marginalised communities. Where both partners were out at work the role of women in the family changed. This was facilitated by the widespread use of contraception and the limitation on the size of families. The EC and organisations like FAS (the Government employment and training authority) encouraged schemes to promote women's return to the work-force. There were some limited resources available for those who wanted to organise women. The focus in the media on problems like the abuse of women and children in the home helped both the women in these communities and those working with them to raise these issues and seek ways of dealing with them.

There was also a growth in the problems which needed to be tackled. Drug and solvent abuse among the young, the decay of local authority housing in inner-city areas, the social consequences of growing unemployment, all forced women to attempt to organise to deal with them. The result has been the mushrooming of a wide range of groups, ranging from those encouraging second-chance education to those campaigning for improvements in the local environment.

For example, in a local authority flat-block estate in west Dublin the tenants' association had fallen into inactivity some twenty years ago. Morale was low and there were many social problems. Then the women started a resource centre to try and tackle the problem of glue sniffing among their children. This developed into a demand for a space for them to meet as women. Tenants' organisations were reactivated as blocks' committees, organised by the women, which cooperated with the local parish council and the local health workers to seek refurbishment of the estate, and a programme for such refurbishment has now been drawn up. Meanwhile the local vocational school has cooperated with the women's group to encourage women to return to education, and several dozen of them have done so. They in turn have become more involved in the community, armed with the self-confidence and articulacy their education has brought them. But the scope of this remains limited, because of the absence of any systematic childcare provision, without which most women with small children cannot participate.[84]

The emergence of these groups has another mainspring – the growing disillusionment with central government, established institutions and political parties. The optimistic dream of the 1970s of full employment and social progress has evaporated. One result has been the growth of alienation and crime, especially amongst the young. Another has been the discovery of a new sense of self-reliance, especially among those members of a community who are most involved in its survival – the women. Throughout both rural and urban Ireland, especially in the most deprived areas, women's groups have sprung up, devoted to personal and community development, tackling a wide range of needs and problems.[85]

These groups are very varied in their objectives and their level of success. But their impact on the way large numbers of Irish women perceive themselves has been considerable – encouraged by the very deliberate patronage of President Robinson, who has singled out such groups for encouragement and praise. Her own attitude to women's issues also seems to have been affected by them, as her speeches on these issues since her election show.

MARY ROBINSON

In her Ogden Lecture to Brown University on 19 October 1991, she offered the following hierarchy of experience: 'through my experience in the home and at my work place and as a member of the Irish Senate, more importantly, through the continual meetings I have had with women right across the political and economic divide in my own country I can confirm that there has never been a more exciting time for a woman to offer her abilities to society.'[86]

She urged her listeners to listen to the stories of the lives of women. 'In the case of women who lived their lives long ago in centuries where disease and prejudice and repression blocked the advancement of women, it can seem that – with some exceptions – we are listening to nothing more than their suffering. But this is not the case. We are also listening to their survival, their achievement of courage, to their tenacity.'[87] She appealed for a review of the past as well as the future.

In her Allen Lane Foundation Lecture on 25 February 1992 President Robinson appealed for a marshalling of the 'new energies and real creative forces which still remain outside the power structures of the established order.' Referring to the women she met in the course of her presidency she said: 'Their ability to devise structures, to order priorities, to assemble an agenda and construe a commitment is not only eloquent. To me it often looks distinctive and creative and therefore a style of problem-solving which is different from the ones we are used to in the public and visible power centres of our society', while she notes that these voices are still not being heard in the power centres.[88]

The visit to West Belfast

Her visit to West Belfast in June 1993 was perfectly consistent with this view. She had been invited by community groups there, to an area which is one of the main centres of support for Sinn Féin in Northern Ireland. She knew perfectly well that it would be impossible to meet real representatives of community organisations there without meeting representatives of and sympathisers with Sinn Féin. Despite considerable pressure against it, her visit went ahead and among the many people she greeted was the president of Sinn Féin and former MP for the area, Gerry Adams. This was met with severe criticism from large sections of the political class throughout the country, though it seems to have done little to dent her popularity with ordinary people.

It is in West Belfast and areas like it in the north of Ireland that the implications of a high level of community organisation can be seen most clearly. There the alienation from the existing power structures has gone further than anywhere else in the country, extending to widespread opposition to and rejection of the authority of the central government. Community movements, built by women in the main, are not only the vehicles through which people try to improve their immediate environment, they are also often the avenues through which they challenge that government.

There is, therefore, a certain convergence of interest between such groups and the political (and also military) movements which oppose that government, here Sinn Féin and the IRA. But to mistake this convergence with identity is to make a great mistake, and ignores the depth and significance of the community-based movements which, in the case of West Belfast, produce a local Irish-language radio station and weekly newspaper and a network of Irish-language nursery schools and a thriving small enterprise centre, as well as a wide range of women's groups involved in more conventional women's activities. Here the full implications of the development of widespread community organisation can be seen, including its implicit opposition to the authority of central government, and President Robinson validated it by her presence. Small wonder that those who are deeply committed to the authority of central governments should have been so disturbed by her actions.

The relationship between community organisation in West Belfast and other nationalist areas in Northern Ireland raises the question of the relationship between nationalism and this kind of organisation. On the one hand the project of nationalism is the creation of a centralised state, based on the nation as perceived by those seeking it. But on the other, where the struggle for this objective is just one part of popular resistance to an oppressive central power, nationalism appears as a unifying ideology for all those involved and therefore is subversive of all authority and plays a decentralising role. In independent Ireland this conflict was resolved by the adoption and reinforcement of the heavily centralised state by the nationalist movement which came to power, and those elements which tended to seek the defusion of power were marginalised.

There is undoubtedly a continued implicit contradiction between a nationalist movement dedicated to the creation of a state and the growth in influence of community-based groups, although a different one from the more often discussed contradiction between the ideologies of republicanism and feminism. This discussion presents republicanism as an essentially patriarchal ideology, and suggests that a feminist consciousness among women will lead them to reject it, despite considerable evidence to the contrary. It ignores the living links between women (as well as men) and their communities and culture, and asks them to deny their culture in order to express themselves as women. The experience of community-based women's groups suggests that women are expressing themselves within their different cultures, while adapting and reinterpreting them.

'The danger of every orthodoxy'

It is clear from the speeches she has made that Mary Robinson has been affected by her experience of meeting women engaged in a wide range of activities in their communities. In another lecture, clearly referring to modern feminism, she urges openness to these other experiences.

> Above all we need to avoid the arrogance which is the danger of every orthodoxy. . . . Feminism . . . [has been about] women getting power over themselves. Nevertheless there is a real danger that we will put too narrow an interpretation on this . . . women who were forced to describe themselves as 'just housewives' –

these are indicators that some women felt excluded on the one hand and, on the other, that a movement which is all about the freedom and excellence and independence of women was marking out some ways of life as appropriate and some as oppressed. . . .

We must never dictate the vision of that life or constrain it by our own narrow interpretation of what is 'right' for women. And I think this applies especially to women of other countries, other faiths, different lifestyles.[89]

This view also applies in this country. Stasia Crickley, who has worked extensively with traveller women, warns against the dangers of this approach.

There is a danger in putting the internal oppression of a community on the agenda. If you say that traveller men are awful you are saying that travellers are awful. This means cultural annihilation. There is a gendered nature to the external oppression such women suffer from. They are blamed for being travellers and for being women, and then for being both without doing anything about it.

The same is true of republican women in the North. The external oppression is what they experience, what forms their lives. The gendered nature of that oppression is that the women suffer if there is no sanitation, if their children are attacked, etc. The space to focus on the liberal agenda [relating to personal liberties, etc] is not there if other things are not equal.

In the North groups focused on things like 'prejudice reduction' have implications for people's views about themselves. Often their agenda is that you need to be strong as women in order to fight your own culture. Women in minority groups do have ways of dealing with their internal oppression within that group, but they have their own way of dealing with it.[90]

Symbol and substance

Her openness to the living traditions of women in Ireland (and elsewhere, especially in the developing world, to which she frequently refers) has greatly enhanced the stature of President Robinson among women in Ireland, especially those who had not followed her career as a lawyer and proponent of women's rights through the legal system before her election. She legitimates their endeavours by her support, but also represents them on the national and international arena, with the multi-faceted role she has developed since her election. She presents herself as a wife and mother (and a partner in a mixed marriage, thereby evoking the pluralism of Ireland's major national and social movements), she is highly educated in a country where education is highly valued, especially for women, and, above all, she represents a kind of politics which appears to transcend personal ambition and power-broking, and appeals to a broader sense of values.

The very nature of the presidency – its largely symbolic role – helps her in this. The fact that the president does not engage in governmental decisions allows Mary Robinson to use the institution to talk about universal aspirations, to use symbols and the language of inclusiveness, as she does in a manner no male politician has been able to do since the foundation of the state. She is thus able to relate to a popular memory of a kind of politics which was about the common good, about general emancipation, about ideals, which has more resonance among the public than the sclerotic system of party politics which came into being with the foundation of the state allows. The very exclusion of women from this system enhances her distinctness from it.

WOMEN AND INSTITUTIONS

Many surveys of official institutions in Ireland show the extent to which they are all dominated by men. Although an unprecedented number of women were elected to the Dáil in the last election, they still number only an eighth of all deputies, approximately the same proportion as there are of local councillors since the 1991 election. In 1991 there were no women at the most senior level in the civil service, no woman Supreme Court judge, no woman Circuit Court judge, and only two women on the High Court.[91]

However, those who seek the solution to the problems of women in Ireland through their increased representation in established institutions may be pursuing a chimera. There is no evidence so far that the increased proportion of women in the Dáil has had any bearing on its legislative programme as all the women there are bound by their respective party's disciplines, and will remain so unless they leave their parties, courting almost inevitable political death. This is likely to remain the case while the current system exists.

This is not necessarily a reason for despondency. Change has mainly been brought about in the modern Irish state, not by the initiative of legislators, but by governmental response to pressure. That pressure comes from lobby groups, of which the most successful are the farmers' associations, businessmen's organisations, the trades unions and the Catholic church. Those representing marginalised groups – and women have been particularly marginalised in this society – have so far been less successful.

THE SECOND COMMISSION ON THE STATUS OF WOMEN

Both the first and second Commissions on the Status of Women involved women's organisations from outside the structures of the state, and as such have offered an opportunity for marginalised groups to make an input into public policy. However, it is unlikely that the Second Commission, any more than the first, will have a profound impact on the lives of the majority of Irish women.

In its guide to its report the Second Commission defined its objective as 'to develop choice and opportunity for women and men and to bring about a fairer gender balance in public life.'[92] What constitutes such choice and opportunity, and just how fair 'fairer' will be, remain undefined.

The general thrust of the report and its recommendations were widely welcomed, including by the Government. However, it is unlikely that many of the recommendations will become a reality in the foreseeable future. Many of them are aspirational, urging changes in social attitudes, to promote, for example, a more equitable distribution of domestic work within the family. It is unlikely that the inclusion of such an exhortation in the Commission's report will persuade men not otherwise inclined to do so to change their behaviour. Other recommendations are so vague as to be virtually meaningless, like the suggestion that the emphasis of social policy should change to enable young single mothers to earn a living rather than be social welfare recipients.

But the most obvious problem with many of the recommendations is their cost. The Commission estimates that a basic childcare development budget, to provide a programme of state-wide childcare, would cost £20 million, not an enormous sum. The recent experience of the Childcare Act is a sobering one. Although passed by the Oireachtas, it languished unimplemented for years on the grounds of cost and it took the tragic case of a young Kilkenny woman abused for over a decade by her father before her case was dealt with by the authorities, to get the commitment for funding for its partial implementation.

Legislation dealing with the most cosmetic aspects of inequality – and some of practical importance, like the joint ownership of the family home – will undoubtedly be implemented, as their cost will be minimal. However, the overwhelming problems of many Irish women are poverty related, and Mary Daly has estimated that a quarter of a million Irish women live in financial poverty.[93] Measures proposed by the Commission relating to women's material circumstances, which are most likely to demand a reallocation of national resources, will depend for their implementation on the existence of a powerful lobby group demanding their implementation. So far no such lobby group exists.

EXTERNAL OPPOSITION

The great movements which have involved women in this country over the past two hundred years have all developed outside the institutions of the existing state, and have usually been opposed to them. This is true of nationalist movements like the United Irishmen, the Fenians and the republican movement of the early years of this century, as well as of social movements like the Ladies' Land League and political movements like the suffrage movement. Women have been accustomed to finding alternative ways of organising and networking. They have fixed their eyes, not on capturing positions within the existing institutions, but on creating different institutions which would be more responsive to the needs of the majority of people, particularly women and children.

This tradition – that of external opposition, of improvisation and experimentation, of finding ways around the institutions of the *status quo* – has been buried deeply, but is not dead. In a fragmented way (and it is, in any case, a decentralised, fragmented tradition) it lives in local women's groups, in *ad hoc* campaigns on specific issues, in the strategies the women of marginalised groups like travellers are finding to articulate their own demands independently both of men in their communities and of well-meaning women from outside their communities.

The challenge for women in Ireland today is to find a way of focusing these initiatives and that energy into a movement powerful enough to force changes in society and in governmental policy. The lessons of those earlier movements, and especially their vision of an alternative type of society to the rigidly hierarchical one created by the men who ran the existing society, will be invaluable in this.

NOTES AND REFERENCES

1. Kumari Jayawardena, *Feminism and Nationalism in the Third World*, London, Zed Books, 1986, p. 100

2. Joanna Liddle and Rama Joshi, *Daughters of Independence: Gender, Caste and Class in India*, London, Zed Books, 1986, p. 34

3. Jayawardena, K. (1986), p. 53

4. Frantz Fanon, *Studies in a Dying Colonialism*, London, Earthscan, 1989, pp. 107–10

5. Christine Obbo, *African Women: Their Struggle for Economic Independence*, London, Zed Press, 1982, pp. 12–14

6. Jawararlal Nehru, *An Autobiography*, Bombay, Asia Publishing House, 1962, quoted in Jayawardena (1986), pp. 98–9

7. Not all European countries are colonisers. Some, like Poland, the Slav nations of central Europe, the Balkans and the nations dominated by Russia were, like Ireland, colonised. For the purposes of contrasting coloniser and colonised I use the term Western Europe to describe the colonising powers of Britain, France, Germany, Belgium, Holland, Spain and Portugal.

8. Benedict Anderson, *Imagined Communities: Reflections on the Origin and Spread of Nationalism*, London, Verso, 1983, p. 19

9. Luke Gibbons, 'Identity without a centre: allegory, history and Irish nationalism' in *Cultural Studies*, volume 6, number 3, October 1992, pp. 360–63

10. Jayawardena, K. (1986), p. 86

11. op. cit., pp. 107–8

12. Mary Wollstonecraft, *A Vindication of the Rights of Women*, London, Everyman, 1992

13. John Finegan, *Anne Devlin: Patriot and Heroine*, Dublin, Elo Publications, 1992, p. 30

14. op. cit., pp. 32–3

15. op. cit., p. 37

16. Luke Gibbons, op. cit., p. 365

17. Maria Luddy, 'Women and Politics in Ireland 1800–1918', unpublished paper given to conference on women in history, Queen's University, Belfast, 27–30 May 1993, p. 2

18. op. cit., p. 3

19. Sylke Lehne, 'The Ladies Committee', chapter in forthcoming thesis on Mary Jane O'Donovan Rossa

20. Lehne, S. 'Fenianism, A Male Business?', chapter in same thesis

21. op. cit.

22. Margaret Ward, *Unmanageable Revolutionaries: Women and Irish Nationalism*, London and Dingle, Pluto Press and Brandon Books, 1983, pp. 15–39

23. Helen Litton (ed.), *Revolutionary Woman: Kathleen Clarke, 1878–1972, An Autobiography*, Dublin, O'Brien Press, 1991, p. 13

24. op. cit., p. 13

25. op. cit., p. 213

26. It was not just in the nationalist movement that women sought ways to avoid and oppose the restrictions society imposed on them. Nuns, domestic servants, women in labouring families, prostitutes and women in workhouses all elaborated their own strategies for survival, usually against the prevailing mores of the time. Equally, women sought a role in society through movements like the temperance movement and the suffrage movement, and it has been the latter which has received most attention to date. See Luddy, Maria and Murphy, Cliona, *Women Surviving: Studies in Irish Women's History in the 19th and 20th Centuries*, Dublin, Poolbeg, 1990, and Owens, Rosemary Cullen, *Smashing Times: A History of the Irish Women's Suffrage Movement 1889–1922*, Dublin, Attic Press, 1984

27. David Lloyd, 'Nationalisms against the State', unpublished paper given to conference on gender and colonialism, University College, Galway, 21–23 May 1992

    See also Carol Coulter, *Ireland: Between the First and the Third Worlds*, Dublin, Attic Press, 1991

28. Mary Colum, *Life and the Dream*, Dublin, Dolmen Press, 1966, p. 96

29. Amanda Sebesteyn, *Prison Letters of Countess Markiewicz*, London, Virago, 1987, p. 37

30. Ward, M. (1983), p. 91

31. Litton, H. (1991), p.69

32. Colum, M. (1966), p. 246

33. Rosemary Cullen Owens, *Smashing Times: A History of the Irish Women's Suffrage Movement 1889–1922*, Dublin, Attic Press, 1984, p. 123

34. Litton, H. (1991), p. 223

35. Owens, R. C. (1984), p. 94

36. Lloyd, D. 'Nationalisms against the State', p. 23

37. Ashis Nandy, *The Intimate Enemy: Loss and Recovery of Self under colonialism*, Delhi, Oxford University Press, 1983, p. 4

38. op. cit., p. 32

39. Mary E. Daly, *Social and Economic History of Ireland since 1800*, Dublin, Educational Company, 1981, p. 173

40. Ward, M. (1983), pp. 163–75

41. See 'Aspects of Women's Contribution to the Oireachtas Debate in the Irish Free State 1922–1937', in Maria Luddy and Cliona Murphy *Women Surviving: Studies in Irish Women's History in the 19th and 20th Centuries*, Dublin, Poolbeg, 1990, pp. 206–32

42. op. cit., pp. 218–221

43. Litton, H. (1991), p. 214

44. For more detail on this see Coulter, C. (1991)

45. Bunreacht na hÉireann (The Irish Constitution), Dublin, Government Publications Office, Article 41

46. Litton, H. (1991) p. 225

47. Hilda Tweedy, *A Link in the Chain: The Story of the Irish Housewives' Association 1942–1992*, Dublin, Attic Press, 1992, p. 15

48. Owens, R. C. (1984)

49. Ward, M. (1983), p. 90

50. op. cit., pp. 142–3

51. op. cit., p. 150

52. Tweedy, H. (1992), p. 13

53. op. cit., p. 7

54. Pat Bolger, (ed.), *And See Her Beauty Shining There: The Story of the Irish Countrywomen*, Dublin, Irish Academic Press, 1986, p. 16

55. Horace Plunkett, Ellice Pilkington and George Russell (AE), *The United Irishwomen: Their Place, Work and Ideals*, Dublin, Maunsel & Co., 1911, p. 1

56. op. cit., p. 68

57. In an interview with the author on 5 April 1993

58. Interview 5 April 1993

59. Interview 5 April 1993

60. Figures from Department of Education

61. Jo Kennedy, 'From "Private" to "Semi-Public" Spheres: Second Chance Education in an Economically Disadvantaged Area in Dublin,' MA thesis, UCD, 1991

62. Jenny Beale, *Women in Ireland: Voices of Change*, Dublin, Gill and Macmillan, 1986, p. 29

63. op. cit., p. 42

64. op. cit., p. 43

65. op. cit., p. 190

66. In an interview with the author 20 May 1993

67. Interview 20 May 1993

68. This is dealt with in more detail in 'Feminism, nationalism and the heritage of the Enlightenment', a paper I gave to a conference on gender and colonialism in University College, Galway, 21–23 May 1992

69. Sonia E. Alvarez, 'Women's Movements and Gender Politics in the Brazilian Transition', in Jane S. Jaquette (ed.), *The Women's Movement in Latin America: Feminism and the Transition to Democracy*, Boston and London, Unwin Hyman, 1989, p. 22

70. Carmen Feigoó, 'The Challenge of Constructing Civilian Peace: Women and Democracy in Argentina', in Jaquette, J. (1989), p. 76

71. Carina Perelli, 'Putting Conservatism to Good use: Women and Unorthodox Politics in Uruguay, from Breakdown to Transition', in Jaquette, J. (1989) p. 102

72. op. cit., p. 105

73. op. cit., p. 107

74. op. cit., p. 108

75. Leila Ahmed, *Women and Gender in Islam: Historical Roots of a Modern Debate*, New Haven and London, Yale University Press, 1992, p. 167

76. op. cit., p. 223

77. op. cit., p. 223

78. op. cit., p. 224

79. Here Ahmed also gives an account of a survey of unveiled and veiled women in Egypt. This showed that a huge majority in both categories (98 per cent of unveiled and 92 per cent of veiled women) approved of education for women. Similar majorities were found in response to questions on women working outside the home and having political

rights. Only in relation to equality within marriage was there a significant difference between the two groups, with a (small) majority of unveiled women for and veiled women against. However, 38 per cent of the veiled women still believed in equality within marriage, although both the *shari'a* (Islamic law) and civil law in Egypt privilege the man in marriage.

80. Kennedy, Jo, 'Sisters, not Saints: Religious Women and Feminism' in *The Irish Reporter*, number 8, fourth quarter 1992

81. Jo Kennedy, in an interview with the author 24 Sept. 1993

82. Information on this and other aspects of Mary Robinson's campaign was given in an interview by Bride Rosney, of Mary Robinson's staff

83. Mulvey, Chris, *Report on the Department of Social Welfare's Grants Scheme for Locally based Women's Groups (1990)*, Combat Poverty Agency, 1991, Research Report Series No. 8

84. Kennedy, Jo, 'From "Private" to "Semi-Public" Spheres: Second Chance Education in an Economically Disadvantaged Area in Dublin', MA thesis, UCD 1991, supplemented by an interview with the author 24 Sept. 1993

85. For a fuller account of such groups, see Mulvey, Chris, op. cit., and Kelleher, Patricia and Whelan, Mary, *Dublin Communities in Action: A Study of Six Projects*, Community Action Network and Combat Poverty Agency, 1992

86. Mary Robinson, 'A Hundred Years – Facing the Challenge', address on the occasion of the Ogden Lecture, Brown University, 19 October, 1991

87. op. cit.

88. Mary Robinson, 'Striking a Balance', The Allen Lane Foundation Lecture, 25 February 1992

89. Mary Robinson, 'A Hundred Years – Facing the Challenge'

90. Stacia Crickley, in an interview with the author, 5 May 1993

91. Galligan, Yvonne, 'Women in Irish Politics', in John Coakley and Michael Gallagher (eds), *Politics in the Republic of Ireland*, Galway, PSAI Press, 1991

92. Second Commission on the Status of Women, *A Guide to the Report*, January 1993, p.5

93. Mary Daly *Women and Poverty*, Dublin, Attic Press, 1989

BIBLIOGRAPHY

Ahmed, Leila, *Women and Gender in Islam: Historical Roots of a Modern Debate*, New Haven and London, Yale University Press, 1992

Anderson, Benedict, *Imagined Communities: Reflections on the Origin and Spread of Nationalism*, London, Verso, 1983

Beale, Jenny, *Women in Ireland: Voices of Change*, Dublin, Gill and Macmillan, 1986

Bolger, Pat, (ed.), *And See Her Beauty Shining There: The Story of the Irish Countrywomen*, Dublin, Irish Academic Press, 1986

Bulbeck, Chilla, *One World Women's Movement*, London, Pluto Press, 1988

Coakley, John and Gallagher, Michael, (eds), *Politics in the Republic of Ireland*, Galway, PSAI Press, 1991

Colum, Mary, *Life and the Dream*, Dublin, Dolmen Press, 1966

Coulter, Carol, *Ireland: Between the First and the Third Worlds*, Dublin, Attic Press, 1990

Coxhead, Elizabeth, *Daughters of Erin: Five Women of the Irish Renascence*, Buckinghamshire, Colin Smith, 1979, first published 1965

Cullen, Mary, 'How radical was Irish feminism between 1860 and 1920?', in Corish, P.J. (ed.), *Radicals, Rebels and Establishments*, Belfast, Appletree, 1985

Daly, Mary, *Social and Economic History of Ireland since 1800*, Dublin, Educational Company, 1981

Daly, Mary, *Women and Poverty*, Dublin, Attic Press, 1989

Fanon, Frantz, *Studies in a Dying Colonialism*, London, Earthscan, 1989

Finegan, John, *Anne Devlin: Patriot and Heroine*, Dublin, Elo Press, 1992

Garvin, Tom, *The Evolution of Irish Nationalist Politics*, Dublin, Gill & Macmillan, 1981

Gibbons, Luke, 'Identity without a centre: allegory, history and Irish nationalism' in *Cultural Studies*, volume 6, number 3, October 1992

Hirsch, Marianne and Keller, Evelyn Fox, *Conflicts in Feminism*, London, Routledge, 1990

Jaquette, Jane S., (ed.), *The Women's Movement in Latin America*, Boston and London, Unwin Hyman, 1989

Jayawardena, Kumari, *Feminism and Nationalism in the Third World*, London, Zed Books, 1986

Kelleher, Patricia and Whelan, Mary, *Dublin Communities in Action*, Dublin, Community Action Network and Combat Poverty Agency, 1992

Kennedy, Jo, 'From "Private" to "Semi Public" Spheres: Second Chance Education in an Economically Disadvantaged Area in Dublin', MA thesis, UCD 1991

Lee, J.J. *Ireland 1945–1970, Thomas Davis Lectures*, Dublin, Gill & Macmillan, 1979

Lehne, Sylke, 'Fenianism – A Male Business', 'The Ladies' Committee' and 'Mary Jane O'Donovan Rossa 1846–1916', all chapters in unpublished thesis on women and fenianism

Liddle, Joanna and Joshi, Rama, *Daughters of Independence: Gender, Caste and Class in India*, London, Zed Books, New Delhi, Kali for Women, 1986

Litton, Helen, (ed.), *Revolutionary Woman: Kathleen Clarke 1878–1972, An Autobiography*, Dublin, O'Brien Press, 1991

Lloyd, David, *Anomolous States: Irish Writing and the Post-Colonial Movement*, Dublin, Lilliput, 1993, and

'Nationalisms against the State: Towards a critique of the Anti-Nationalist Prejudice', unpublished paper delivered in Galway in May 1992

Luddy, Maria, 'Women and Politics in Ireland 1800–1918', unpublished paper delivered in Belfast May 1993

Meany, Gerardine, *Sex and Nation: Women in Irish Culture and Politics*, Dublin, Attic Press, 1991

Mulvey, Chris, *Report on the Department of Social Welfare's Grants Scheme for Locally Based Women's Groups (1990)*, Dublin, Combat Poverty Agency, 1991

Nandy, Ashis, *The Intimate Enemy: Loss and Recovery of Self Under Colonialism*, Delhi, Oxford University Press, 1983

Obbo, Christine, *African Women: Their Struggle for Economic Independence*, London, Zed Press, 1982

Omvedt, Gail, *We Will Smash This Prison: Indian Women in Struggle*, London, Zed Press, 1980

Owens, Rosemary Cullen, *Smashing Times: A History of the Irish Women's Suffrage Movement 1889–1922*, Dublin, Attic Press, 1984

Parker, Andrew; Russo, Mary; Sommer, Doris and Yaeger, Patricia, (eds), *Nationalisms and Sexualities*, New York and London, Routledge, 1992

Pateman, Carole, *The Disorder of Women: Democracy, Feminism and Political Theory*, Cambridge, Polity Press, 1989

Pyle, Jean Larson, *The State and Women in the Economy: Lessons from Sex Discrimination in the Republic of Ireland*, New York, State University and New York Press, 1990

Ramazanoglu, Caroline, *Feminism and the Contradictions of Oppression*, London, Routledge, 1989

Robinson, Mary, 'A Hundred years – Facing the Challenge', address by President Mary Robinson on the occasion of the Ogden Lecture, Brown

University, 19 October 1991 and 'Striking a Balance', the Allen Lane Foundation Lecture, 25 February 1992

Sebestyen, Amanda, (ed.), *Prison Letters of Countess Markiewicz*, London, Virago, 1987

Second Commission on the Status of Women, *Report*, January 1993, and *A Guide to the Report*, January 1993

Tabari, Azar and Yeganeh, Nahid, *In the Shadow of Islam: The Women's Movement in Iran*, London, Zed Books, 1982

Tweedy, Hilda, *A Link in the Chain: The Story of the Irish Housewives' Association 1942–1992*, Dublin, Attic Press, 1992

Ward, Margaret, *Unmanageable Revolutionaries: Women and Irish Nationalism*, London, Pluto Press, 1983 and *Maud Gonne: Ireland's Joan of Arc*, London, Unwin Hyman, 1990

Wollstonecraft, Mary, *A Vindication of the Rights of Women*, London, Everyman, 1992